Read the Way You Talk

A Guide for Lectors

Jack Hartjes

Jack Hartjes

LITURGICAL PRESS

Collegeville, Minnesota

www.litpress.org

To the dedicated lectors at St. Paul's Parish,
including Roseanna Ross,
whose help and encouragement are appreciated.

Cover design by Greg Becker

1   2   3   4   5   6   7   8

Library of Congress Cataloging-in-Publication Data

Hartjes, Jack.
    Read the way you talk : a guide for lectors / Jack Hartjes.
      p. cm.
    Includes bibliographical references.
    ISBN 0-8146-2972-5 (alk. paper)
    1. Reading in public worship. 2. Lay readers—Catholic Church.
  I. Title.

BX1915.H37 2004
264'.02034—dc22

2003054644

Contents

Preface

This is a how-to book for lectors, deacons, priests—anyone who works at sharing the Word of God with others, especially at the Sunday Liturgy. It takes skill to read aloud, and practice is the way to improve at it. This guidebook can help make your practice more effective.

Here you will find more detailed instructions than in many guides for readers, describing what to do and how to do it, in eighteen different areas. Compared to other guides, some of the instructions are new, some are different, and all have a unique focus. The guidance presented here follows from the key conviction that reading should be "like talk"—like telling someone what's on your mind. This guide shows how to make oral reading not only meaningful but also believable. Its various instructions will help you plan and practice so you can do what comes naturally when you just talk, when you are comfortable with your audience, sure of what you are saying, and confident that your story or message is interesting or important for your listeners. The result will be a reading that conveys meaning better and sounds more like something you really mean to say.

I have lectored and worked with other readers at Catholic liturgies for twenty years. An even larger part of my "résumé" has been reading out loud with my children at home and with my students as an elementary school teacher. That I now feel I have something to say to other readers is due also to Dr. Josephine Callan. She taught courses in the speech and drama department of The Catholic University of America. Her favorite saying "Read like talk" has guided all my oral reading, whether in church, in class, or at home. I realized that I must be having some success in applying my teacher's lesson when I came down the stairs one day and my wife asked me, "Who were you talking to up there?" I'd been sitting with our daughter on the top step reading a story.

People come alive when they talk, and that sparkle, conviction, and variety—that humanness—belong to the celebration of the Word of God with the people of the word. A brief theological reflection in Part 1 of this resource explains why. The much larger Part 2, the working part of the book, has rules, explanation of techniques, and examples designed to help you read like talk.

Reading that sounds like talk is not easy. Talking is natural to us, and reading may be second nature to some, but you have to work to make oral reading sound like talk. After learning and practicing out loud a few rules and techniques presented here, it would be a good idea to apply them to some Sunday readings—maybe the Sunday you will read next. For this purpose Part 2 is in three lessons with the most important ideas in Lesson 1. You don't need to know everything to get started. Gradually, the practice of reading that is "like talk" becomes almost, but not quite, a habit.

PART 1

The Word of God
in Human Speech

The reading of the Word of God in church should sound like talk. That is the guiding principle of this resource. Helping you read like talk is its goal. But why should the Word of God sound like talk? Even if "reading like talk" is good policy for other situations, does that mean it's right for the readings of the Liturgy of the Word? To answer this question, it will help to understand what is new about the Catholic Church's celebration of the Word of God since the Second Vatican Council.

The Council instituted a marvelous change in Catholics' experience of the Word of God. Protestant Churches had done it, and in the Catholic Church it was developing over a period of time, not just a creature of the 1960s. The Council put its seal of approval on the movement to make the Word of God available to everyone in the language of the people. It made no exception for the Church's official public celebrations, "the work of the people," the liturgy. The Word of God lives, not in a dead language spoken quietly to God by the priest while the rest of the people get the translated word silently from missals, but in the very minds and lives of the people who have come together to celebrate that word.

People celebrate the Word of God, and both the celebration and the word itself belong to the people. These basic facts help us understand what the Liturgy of the Word is like as well as what it is not like. First, it is not like a meditation, something that can be done just as well silently and individually. Not an individual exercise with a

1

book, but a celebration, something people do together, with members of the community taking leadership roles—that's what the Liturgy of the Word is. If possible, even those who cannot hear the spoken word because of hearing impairment should have a chance to celebrate along with the community by means of a simultaneous translation into sign language. Second, the reading of the Word of God in liturgy is not like a lesson, and the reader is not like a teacher giving knowledge to people who didn't have it before. Rather, the word belongs to the people all along, even before they hear it at liturgy. It is their words, their stories. They come together to hear them once again not—at least not primarily—because they forgot some of it but mainly because they like hearing it again and again.

That is the attitude that the reader must take. You are there to help the community celebrate its own stories. The community loves its stories, and you must enjoy reading them. The community is energized by its stories, and some of that energy must come from the way you read. The community is called to account by its stories, and that call must sound through your voice. The community is brought face to face with the marvelous message and work of God in its stories, so the reading needs a spirit of awe and wonder, a you-are-there quality. In short, you must read the way you imagine the text's human author would have told the story or spoken the message the first time.

Reading like talk, as opposed to reading that sounds like a book, has huge advantages. People can understand and remember the message better because it's the kind of language they're accustomed to. People can believe the message more easily because it sounds as if the reader actually believes it. When reading sounds like words from a book, even if the words are competently spoken, the meaning may not be there, or it may not be presented in the way people are used to hearing. Then the listeners have to stop, think, and figure it out. That's a big disadvantage. The freshness and power of God's Word come from hearing it, not from taking it apart and putting it back together again.

The mystery of the incarnation is here: God became fully human and God's message was spoken to people in ordinary human language. That is the theology behind the change from Latin to the language of the people, and it is the theological reason why the reading of the Word of God in church should sound as natural as possible. It should be something we can relate to. It should be in our first language. It should be "like talk."

PART 2

Rules for Reading Like Talk

Introduction

Reading the Word of God isn't just reading words. It's telling a message or a story. I like the word *telling* because it's something we do all the time. It's a word that sets us on the path to understanding how to do it, and, unlike another good word, *proclaiming*, it's not likely to be translated as "reading very loud." Reading aloud is a way for somebody to tell somebody something, and it should sound like that, with all the intensity and variety of feeling that happens when people talk.

Over the years I have identified rules and techniques that are at work when reading sounds like talk, and I have taught them to others. Books for lectors commonly cover a wide range of topics, including preparation, understanding the text, diction, pacing and pauses, volume, expressing emotion, eye contact, and using the microphone. This guide is more narrowly focused. It deals in one way or another with most of these topics, but only as they become important in the work of making your reading sound as it would if you were telling an idea or a story and not just reading words out loud.

The following material is divided into eighteen rules for reading like talk spread out over three lessons. Examples illustrate each of the rules, and it will be most useful to you to read these examples aloud. Lesson 1 is the most important. When you are finished with that, it's time to dig into some actual readings from the Lectionary or your Bible and work on applying those techniques. Come back to the other lessons later.

Each rule is meant to help you read with greater understanding, more convincingly, more like saying what's on your mind and less like—well—reading. Learning the rules, however, is not a final goal to reach and be satisfied with. Even with the rules in hand, there are challenges. There are times when the rules are hard to apply, when some disagreement can be expected. There are judgment calls and exceptions that I'm not sure I can explain— although, many times when I've wanted to make an exception, I've found, after a bit of thought, that the rule does work, after all. Following the rules isn't all there is to reading well. Most important is the need to find your own natural voice and become comfortable telling confidently the message you really do believe.

LESSON 1

The Heart of the Matter: Communication

The Liturgy of the Word belongs to the people, but that doesn't change the fact that the Word of God is sometimes hard to understand. When you talk, on the other hand, you do understand what you are saying. A lot of things, like pace and pauses and patterns of pitch, go right simply because the thoughts you speak are your own. Also one more thing is going on to help your listeners get the message. When you are communicating, you take into account the point of view of the listener and how the listener's perceptions change as the conversation goes on. Because of that you are able, automatically, to stress the words that the listener needs to pay attention to most.

The change that occurs in the listeners is a factor that often is left out of instructions for readers. You are told to work at understanding the text and then emphasize the important ideas, emphasize verbs and nouns. That advice is too abstract. You need to factor in the relationship between the ideas and the listeners, the ones for whom these ideas are important. When you talk, you don't weigh the importance of ideas in the abstract. You don't put verbs ahead of nouns and nouns ahead of adjectives and so on. When you are talking and not reading, an entirely different kind of weighing goes on in some corner of your mind. It's automatic, and it runs something like this: You know your listener. You have a pretty good idea of what your listener is thinking about to start with, and, most important, you have a kind of automatic counter in your mind that keeps track of everything that either of you says. It's in this constantly changing context that, without thinking about it, you determine which words to stress and which to pronounce without stress. Whether a word is a verb, a noun, or an adjective hardly counts at all. (That's the way it works in English, anyway. Some other languages work differently, and that is part of the reason for the interesting, foreign sound of the English speech of people whose native language is Spanish, for example. Spanish word emphasis follows a different rule.)

In the Liturgy of the Word you have a few minutes to communicate the Word of God to the assembled people, and that means doing your best to make it easy to understand. When you are preparing to do that, you first try to understand the text yourself, but then you take the point of view of the listeners. You ask over and over, "What do the listeners need to pay special attention to now?" That is the main thing I think about when I am preparing a reading, and I think about it at every step, every sentence, along the way. It's not just for a few main ideas. I believe that taking care of the needs of your listeners all along is a better strategy than looking for that single most important idea to emphasize. If your text has a climax or main idea, it will promote itself when it comes. Meanwhile, often some listener will have been moved deeply by God's grace speaking through a smaller detail in another part of the story.

Every sentence in a reading has words that require the listeners' special attention and words that don't, words that you would stress if you were just talking and words that you wouldn't. Preparing a reading takes effort. You have to plan so you can stress the right words. That is the largest part of making reading sound "like talk." There's more to it than that, but getting the stresses right also helps with some of the other things—like pace and pauses and pitch.

Right and Wrong or Just a Matter of Style?

I am proposing rules for making your reading sound like talk. It's not just a matter of sounding better. Rather, it's the power with which the Word of God is communicated. It's how convincing you are as the messenger. It's even whether the listeners will be able to understand what you read. Or will they have to think hard before what you just read makes sense to them and run the risk of missing what's coming next? The way you read, especially the stresses you use, can even change the meaning of a text.

These rules are a framework. They are part of what makes our speech English. Within the framework there is room for differences in style and room to grow. I went to a high school play and must have caught the enthusiasm with which the young people spoke their lines. The next time I came to the Word of God, I found that I was reading differently. I hadn't changed any rules, but I grew some. I have heard professional readers who seemed to be following all these same rules—whether consciously or not—and yet the reading they produced was completely different from anything I would, or could, have done. That is style. The right way to read is "like talk." Your personal style is another matter, and everyone has his or her own style of talking.

Any one person talks differently in different situations. Sometimes you talk excitedly. Sometimes you tell a story with dramatic effect. There are pleading, cajoling, warning, informing, and many other ways of talking, practically all of which can be found in the Bible. Reading like talk does not reduce the variety of ways to present the Word of God—just the opposite.

How do you get reading to sound like talk? When you are talking, especially when you are relaxed and sure of yourself and comfortable with your listeners, the thoughts come already embodied in words, and the right emphases, the right feelings, the right sense of drama come automatically. When you are reading, there is a struggle with the words themselves, the thoughts are not your own, and there is no give-and-take with another person. Nothing comes automatically. How do you know which words to stress? Besides word stress, what else is involved in reading that is "like talk"? The sections that follow contain rules and examples to show you what I have learned about reading like talk.

The rules are not the main thing. When you are applying these rules, keep hold of this basic idea: It has to sound like talk. You should listen to yourself read out loud and see if you can imagine yourself talking like that. With the printed word in front of you, though, sometimes it's hard to imagine what real talking is like. These rules can help you remember. Spoken English is the basic reality, and the rules describe it. It's your way of talking that counts most when you are the reader.

RULE 1: Use the Downward Inflection

To say that reading should be like talk is not quite specific enough. Reading the Word of God should be like the kind of talking we do when we are confident about what we are saying. As a teacher I sometimes ask questions only to have the students "ask" me the answer. They know the answer, but they don't believe they can just say it. What I hear is "The Declaration of Independence?" when what I'm looking for is "The Declaration of Independence!"

Something like that goes on—often needlessly, I think—in ordinary conversation as well. Someone says something but at the same time seems to be communicating, "I could be wrong about this. I'm not presuming that you have to believe this." Or else it's an overly polite "Is it O.K. with you if I say this?" Sometimes it's "I'm not confusing you, am I?" or "Is this the right word?" You'll hear the speaker's voice rising in pitch at various points almost like a series of questions.

This first rule of reading like talk insists: Say it, don't ask it. We want to sound as if we are sure our message is true and worth someone else's close attention. The way to make your speech sound like something you really mean and something important is to use the downward inflection often. I have heard of presidents taking lessons on the downward inflection so that they can sound as if they know what they are talking about.

Downward inflection means going from a higher to a lower pitch. Here are some other important things to remember about the downward inflection:

- It is not just for the ends of sentences, where most readers do use it. There are many places throughout a sentence where a downward inflection is appropriate.
- It is not at all a lower-energy kind of reading, like coming to a rest, which is something that readers do too often to the ends of sentences.
- The downward inflection, moving from a higher to a lower pitch, happens most often within a single word, often all on one syllable.
- Most of the phrases in most sentences should end with a downward inflection.
- Some downward inflections don't go all the way down, and some end with a very slight upward movement. That tells the listener that the current thought is completed by what immediately follows.

A punctuation mark or the end of a line in the Lectionary usually indicates the end of a phrase, where most often there should be a downward inflection. In the following passage I used the vertical bar (|) to mark the ending of some other phrases, other places for a downward inflection. The chart after the passage is an attempt at a visual expression of what the downward inflection sounds like. Unfortunately, it doesn't come near to showing the variety of pitches that people use in conversation; not all downward inflections are alike. The chart does show that there are a lot of them. It shows several instances where the higher and the lower pitches are on one accented syllable. Other times the higher pitch is on an accented syllable and the lower pitch is on the unaccented syllables or words that follow. The inflections that

end with a slight upward movement are marked with an arrow (^)
in the chart.

> [H]e shall proclaim peace | to the nations.
> His dominion | shall be from sea to sea,
>   and from the River to the ends of the earth.
> As for you, for the blood of your covenant with me,
>   I will bring forth your prisoners | from the dungeon
> (Zech 9:10-11).

Use this chart to get an approximate picture of these downward
inflections:

claim pe-
he shall pro-
        eace
	na-
	to the
	    tions

min-
his do-
    ion^
	sea to se-
	shall be from
	      ea

River ends of the er- and from the to the earth.	

yoo-
As for
   ou^
	blood cov-
	for the of your
	      enant with me^,

bring forth   pris-
I will   your
      oners
	dun-
	from the
	    geon.

Notice that no individual words have an upward inflection.
It's either flat or down at the end. You might think a straight upward swing on *dominion* in the second line and on some other
words sounds really nice. But here's one more important point
about the downward inflection: Its opposite is too tempting. The
upward inflection has only a couple uses. In actual talk, except
when people are not confident or comfortable, it's rather rare.

If you let yourself feel the mood of a reading, you'll use lots
of pitches, just like talk. Work at making use of three options:

Some words or phrases higher in pitch, some words or phrases lower, and some individual words with the downward inflection, going from high to low on one word. The fourth option, going from low to high on a word is often tempting, especially when you're trying not to read in a monotone; but generally avoid this one. Later rules will describe two special situations where the upward inflection belongs.

The downward inflection does not mean that a word gets less energy. These are stressed words, and you change to a lower pitch only after beginning the word on a higher pitch, even for the one-syllable words and even if it's the last word in the sentence. All these words with more than one pitch get a great deal of energy.

When reading, be bold, be sure. Once, after lectoring, I was told, "You must really believe what you read." That compliment aimed higher than it needed to. If I sound as if I really believe what I'm reading, it's not because I have more faith than another. It's because . . .

> I have lear-   use   downward inflec-
>   rned | to   the   tion.

RULE 2: Say It. Don't Sing It

It's important not to read in a monotone. Most of us use a wide variety of pitches when we talk. People whose voices are what we call musical are the most pleasant to listen to. Even the most musical way of speaking, however, is completely different from singing. What I call singing is a pattern that unwary readers tend to fall into that has nothing to do with spoken English or the meaning of any text ever written. It's a monotonous rising and falling, rising and falling, like a predictable melody, usually settling down quietly at the ends of sentences. Here's the wrong way to read part of the passage quoted above in Rule 1:

>   ver
>   Ri-   ends of the
> from the   to the   er-
>   earth.

It starts out with an upward movement and lots of energy, modulates to a middle pitch for "ends of the," then settles down peacefully at the end. Practically all the other lines in that passage could be read the same up and back down way, and it's a pattern that you hear often in reading that does NOT sound like talk. In natural speech, changes in pitch happen often, suddenly and almost any place in a sentence. There is no one repeated melody. Volume and speed also change to convey different levels of importance or excitement, and sentences often get exciting and important right at the very end—as in the next passages. Bold type indicates words the listeners need to pay special attention to:

If by the **spirit** I you **put to death** I the **deeds** of the **body,** you will **live** (Rom 8:13).

Unclean spirits, crying out in a **loud voice,**
came out of **many** • **possessed** • **people,**
and many **paralyzed** or **crippled** people were **cured.**
There was **great joy** in that city (Acts 8:7-8).

Only the last sentence—where *joy* gets the most stress and *in that city* is lower in both volume and pitch—is one that settles down quietly at the end. All the other lines end with hard-hitting words that need both a high and a low pitch, a downward inflection, and lots of energy.

In this passage and in most of the examples that follow there are no raised or lowered letters but there are cues for the downward inflection. And there are two other cues that I use regularly to indicate how to read:

• First, **vertical bars** indicate the ends of phrases, or places to pause. Usually—not quite always—the ends of phrases need a downward inflection, but they are not the only places. I would also use a downward inflection on the word *paralyzed* in this passage. Commas generally indicate a pause and a downward inflection, and so—usually—do the ends of lines as the Lectionary formats them. I don't put the vertical bar where there's a comma or at the end of a line.

- Second, **bold type** indicates words the listener needs to hear most. Stress these; raise the volume. Pronounce the other words clearly, but in the background. Knowing which words to stress is the most important part of making your reading sound like talk.
- Finally, I put a dot between two stressed words when they need a **slight • separation**. Perhaps the two words represent unrelated ideas or maybe they contribute to a whole but the separate parts are individually important and it's hard to hear that without a bit of separation. In the above passage *many • possessed • people* is like this. Other phrases are just the opposite. They need to be read almost as one word, so I put the whole phrase in bold print without separators. *Put to death* is an example of this.

Reading with a repeating pattern is a sure way not to sound like natural speech. It's a common habit also. You can break this habit by paying close attention to words that need stress. As soon as you start applying the next couple rules on when and when not to stress, you will find that words that need stress sometimes bunch close together, and sometimes they're few and far between. There are a lot of them, and they come with absolutely no regularity. It will be almost impossible to maintain any kind of singsong pattern. Paying attention to all those stresses will also help you avoid the monotone style of reading.

RULE 3: Don't Stress Unimportant Words

The often repeated advice about emphasizing important ideas should be rephrased negatively. Turned around it has more limited application, but, it will help you avoid some common mistakes. Almost, but not quite, any word can be—in some instance or another—a word that the listener needs to pay special attention to. This negative rule eliminates a few categories of words that never, or almost never, are that important. Here is a list with instructions on when to stress each category:

Category	When to stress
Articles—a, an, the	Never (and don't say "a" with a long *ay* sound).
Helping verbs—will, am, is, are, can, might, should, have . . . (with another verb)	Almost never unless the main verb is stressed. (*Does, do,* and *did* are exceptions.)
Conjunctions—and, or, but, when, because, if	Once in a great while.
Prepositions—in, to, with, against . . .	Sometimes, but not nearly as often as you'd probably like.

Even experienced readers often make the mistake of emphasizing these unimportant words, especially the prepositions. Here are two examples with the stress in the correct places. (I've underlined the prepositions, but don't stress them.)

I will **put** my **spirit** in you | that you may **live** (Ezek 37:14). *(In* isn't doing a very big job here. We know what the sentence means even if we miss that word.)

[U]pon **this rock** I will **build** my **church,** and the **gates** of the **netherworld** | shall not **prevail** against it (Matt 16:18). (How else can you prevail except "against" something? You don't need to stress *against.* It's too obvious.)

Most prepositions don't add much to what the reader understands even before hearing them, but *put, spirit, this rock,* and *prevail* do. Stress these words.

Sometimes a preposition needs emphasis because it's different from what one might expect or because it's the only important word around:

I will be **with** you | and **bless** you. . . (Gen 26:3).

Some prepositions are stressed because they aren't functioning as prepositions but are part of a verb that is stressed:

[T]he LORD will be **passing by** (1 Kgs 19:11).
[W]hoever does not **take up** his **cross**
and **follow after** me | is not **worthy** of me (Matt 10:38).

The little conjunctions *and*, *but*, and *or* make another group of words that you hardly ever stress. They hardly ever contain what is new. Here's a rare example where one of these words does:

And do not be **afraid** of those who **kill** the **body** | but
  cannot kill the **soul;**
rather, be afraid of the one who can destroy
both soul **and** body | in **Gehenna** (Matt 10:28).

There are many kinds of words that can make a big difference in a sentence. They can be found in any part of a sentence. How do you know which ones the listener needs to pay special attention to, which ones to stress? The next rule is your most important guide. It is the rule I have to think about all the time when I am preparing a reading.

RULE 4: Stress New Information

Did you notice in the previous passage that long stretch after the word *rather* without any stresses? That's because nothing there was new for the listeners. Keeping track of information you give is the way you keep up with your listeners' changing awareness. Stressing what's new is the most important rule for reading like talk. Actually, it includes the previous rule. After all, the reason we don't emphasize words like *a*, *an*, and *the* is that they don't contain much, if anything, in the way of information. But many words do express information. They come anywhere in a reading, usually several in one sentence. I'm not thinking of the point of a story or of major ideas that an author wants to communicate, and I don't mean words that are important in the abstract. God is arguably the most important idea in the Bible, but that doesn't mean you always stress the word *God*. This rule says stress the new information—a person or thing, an action, a quality— anything that a word can represent.

Many new readers tend to read too fast. If you pay attention to words that contain information, however, and stress all the words that contain new information, it's very hard to race. Try this reading in the left column below. Stress the words in bold print. On the right I explain what exactly is new about each of these words.

Here's the reading:	**Here's what being "new" means:**
Then **Peter**	**stood up**	with the **eleven,**	Peter and the eleven haven't been mentioned before, and no one has stood up before.
raised his voice, and **proclaimed:**	We don't know about any voices being raised or any proclaiming going on before this point.
"Let the **whole** • **house of Israel**	**know** for **certain**	We haven't thought about any whole things or about the house of Israel yet; no one has known anything for certain yet.
that **God**	has **made** him both **Lord** and **Christ**	This is the first mention of God or of making or of anyone's being either Lord or Christ.
this **Jesus** whom you **crucified**" (Acts 2:14, 36).	Jesus is mentioned here for the first time; we haven't heard about anyone being crucified yet.

In this reading practically every noun and verb and even an adjective and an adverbial phrase contain new things that need to be stressed.

The following paragraph has a very different rhythm:

"**Come** to me, all you who **labor** | and are **burdened,**
and I will **give** you **rest.**
Take my **yoke** upon you | and **learn** from me,
for I am **meek** | and **humble of heart;**
and you will **find • rest** for yourselves.
For my yoke is **easy,** and my **burden • light**" (Matt 11:28-30).

Not stressing is just as important as stressing for helping the listener understand. By the time Jesus speaks the last line, he knows that his listeners already have the idea of a yoke in their minds, so he doesn't stress that word again. He stresses what's new, namely, that it's easy.

Burden in the last line isn't exactly a new word because the idea is there in the first line, but clearly it needs to be stressed. That complicates the rule about new information a little. A repeated item counts as new if in between or nearby there occurs another item that is enough like the first that it competes with it for the listener's attention. In this case *yoke* comes between the first and the second mention of *burden*. You have to stress the second *burden* to get the listener's attention back away from *yoke*.

Here's an example with several repetitions that need to be stressed. They are underlined.

For the **gifts** | and the **call** | of **God** | are **irrevocable.**
Just as **you** • **once** • **disobeyed** God
but have now **received mercy** | because of **their** [the Gentiles']
    disobedience,
so **they** have now disobeyed | in order that,
by virtue of the mercy shown to **you,**
they too may now receive mercy (Rom 11:29-31).

One's attention has to shift over and over between Gentiles and Jews. To accomplish the shifts, the listener needs help to pay special attention to some of the same words over and over. These words are: *you*, *their,* and *they.* On the other hand, the word *mercy*, which occurs three times in the last four lines, needs to be stressed only once because there is nothing else like mercy that anyone is receiving. It's the same with *disobeyed* and *disobedience.* If you stress these words more than once, you begin to hide the contrast in the words *you*, *they,* and *their.*

Finding and stressing what is new is one of the first things you do as you prepare a reading to make it sound like talk. It's the basic rule on what to stress. Its corollary is next.

RULE 5: Leave Some Words Unstressed

In a typical reading there are many ideas, and each new idea adds to the complexity of the passage. Your listener needs some help, and the first thing you do is stress whatever is new. But the second thing is just as important. The listener will understand what you are reading more easily if you avoid stressing words that do not need it.

Words in a sentence that you do not stress are the ones with no surprises, nothing new. They are the easiest for listeners to understand. Don't worry that people won't be able to follow you when you lower the volume. In fact, your listeners will have a harder time understanding you if you don't lower the volume on these words because then they will sound like new information and compete with all the other really new things. As the reader and first interpreter of the text, you shouldn't leave all the work of sorting that out to your listeners. You do need to pronounce these words clearly, but lowered volume and, often, increased speed in these parts actually aid the listeners' understanding. Notice all the words that are not stressed in this example:

> You **duped** me, O LORD, and I **let** myself be duped
> (Jer 20:7).

No one expressing this thought in an actual conversation would ever stress the last word. Try it. Substitute the name of someone you know for "O LORD" and use a more common word like *tricked* for *duped*. In conversation we don't stress repeated ideas.

Sometimes you will find words that aren't exactly repetitions, but what they add does not matter to the thought being communicated. Most or all of what they express is implied in the rest of the sentence. After the story in which Jesus cures many possessed, paralyzed, and crippled people, the author states:

> There was **great joy** in that city (Acts 8:8).

I didn't stress *city*. The event had to happen somewhere. The fact that it was in a city doesn't make any difference. Here's an unusual passage with four of these implied ideas:

> "He has **raised up** a **horn** for our **salvation**
>   within the **house of David** his **servant**,
>   even as he **promised** through (1) the mouth of his **holy**
>   **prophets** from of **old:**
>   . . . to **show mercy** to our **fathers**
>   and to be **mindful** of his **holy covenant**
>   and of the **oath** (2) he swore to **Abraham** our father. . . .
>   to **guide** our **feet** into (3) the **path** of **peace**."
>   . . . and he was in the **desert** until (4) the day of his
>   **manifestation** to **Israel** (Luke 1:69-80).

None of these four phrases adds anything new. Promising is done with the mouth, oaths are always sworn, feet have to travel on a path, and everything happens on some day or other. I still chose to stress *path* in the third phrase. Without it, it's hard to make the connection between feet and peace.

Stressing all the words that contain new information and not stressing old ideas is the primary way to get meaning across. It's what we do when we talk. For those in-between words that don't make much difference because they express little other than what is implied already, stressing is somewhat optional, but readings from Scripture are full of meaningful words. You are kinder to the listener if you don't stress more than you need to.

Now is a good time to go to some Mass readings or a Bible and practice some of the rules for reading like talk. As you do, be sure to: use the downward inflection often, avoid a regular up-and-down pattern of pitches, stress new information, and avoid stressing old information and unimportant words like most prepositions.

LESSON 2

A certain way of speaking comes naturally to us, but there is not much natural about reading aloud. Getting it right, however, not only makes a reading sound good; it also helps your listener understand what you are reading. There are rules that can guide you, including the five in Lesson 1. Some are habits you can develop—like the downward inflection. Others never stop needing constant watchfulness, chief among these being Rule 4, finding what is new in each sentence and stressing that. All of the rules are designed to make your reading sound as natural as talking, to make it sound, as Rule 2 says, like saying as opposed to singing.

The next set of rules starts with one that I find I need to think about quite often. It tells how to read items in a series—something that is so common that it seems it must be really simple; but there is a trick to it.

RULE 6: Don't Sing Items in a Series

Series of items are very common in the Bible and in conversation. (A series can be just two.) This is a time when the temptation to "sing," or use an inappropriate pattern of pitches, is really strong. Readers often raise the pitch of the first item of a series, coast through the middle (if there are more than two), and lower the pitch on the last item, and that's usually wrong. This up and down pattern actually has a definite meaning. It says that the list is a complete one. Examples would be when the twelve apostles are being named or when St. Paul tells about the three things that last:

>   **aith,**
> **fai-**   **hope,** and   (1 Cor 13:13)
>   **love**

The upward inflection on *faith* works here. But usually items in a series are just some of the possibilities. The author is not trying to tell you all of them. In these cases, don't think of the series as having . . .

>   ginning,
> a be-   a middle, and an
>   end

that need to be distinguished by the way you use your voice. Think of each item separately, as if it were the only one, and pronounce it that way. Stress each with the emphasis that it deserves, not necessarily all the same. Reading items in a series correctly, since these are so common in the Bible, is a large part of the way I avoid that singsong reading pattern. Be careful to use the downward inflection on all of the items if it's not a complete list. Don't lose energy on the last item, even if it ends the sentence.

    In the next examples the items in series are shown with raised and lowered letters to indicate the downward inflection, but they are not the only ones that should have a downward inflection.

> [G]ive to the LORD glo-   and pra-   (1 Chr 16:28).
>   ry   aise

>   ry
> (Not glo-   and pra-
>   aise.)

rich-   wis-   knowl-

Oh, the depth of the   God!

           es I and   dom I and   edge of

(Rom 11:33).

     es

(Not rich-   and wisdom and know-

                    ledge.)

A slight pause between items in a series usually is a good idea. Don't die out on *God* in this last passage; give it its own two-note downward inflection.

A series doesn't have to be nouns. It can be two or more verbs or other parts of speech as well:

[C]ome, **receive** • **grain** and **eat;**
Come, **without paying** I and without **cost,**
drink • **wine** and **milk!** (Isa 55:1).

Each line contains a different two-item series. None of them is a complete list. Read each item with a downward inflection. I made my decision to pause after *paying,* and I probably would not pause after *Come* in the second line, in spite of the comma, but others might decide differently.

A series of two opposites or a series that includes the words "both . . . and . . ." often has the quality of a complete list.

                Lord

God has **made** both   **Chri-**

                and   **ist,**

this **Jesus** whom you **crucified**" (Acts 2:36).

A series of items that make a complete list can go up in pitch on the first item and down on the last. But most series are not complete. The basic rule for items in a series that is not complete is: Pronounce each item as you would if it were the only one in the list. Use the downward inflection. That gives an item its own identity and helps separate it from the others. A slight pause between items often helps. It enhances this sense of separate identity.

RULE 7: Stress the Second Half of Comparisons and Parallelisms

Instructions for oral reading commonly tell you to emphasize comparisons or contrasts and parallel constructions, but how to do it is not stated. That's leaving out a lot. To make a comparison, contrast, or parallelism clear, always stress its second half. These are the procedures in more detail:

Comparisons and contrasts. You rarely need to give any special stress to the first of the compared or contrasted items just because it has a partner coming up soon. Treat the first the way you would when following other rules. For example, stress it if it's new. But do stress the second item, no matter what.

Parallelisms. Usually there are four items. The relationship between the first two is compared to the relationship between two other items or between the same two in reverse order. Stress either or both of the first pair if required by other rules, but always stress both of the second pair.

Here are two examples of contrasts and three of parallelisms. The underlining shows the contrasted or parallel items. Stress these words only if they are also in bold print.

CONTRAST 1:

You have **seen** for **yourselves** | how I **treated** the **<u>Egyptians</u>** and how I **bore • <u>you</u> • up** | on **eagle** wings . . . (Exod 19:4).

You in the second line is contrasted with Egyptians. It's easy to miss the stress on *you* because it's such a small word. Actually it needs more stress than either *bore* or *up*. Separate it a little. (Notice the dots around *you*.)

CONTRAST 2:

Now I am **speaking** to you **Gentiles.**
Inasmuch then as I am the **apostle** to the Gentiles,
I **glory** in my ministry I in order to make **my race jealous** . . .
(Rom 11:13-14).

In the second and third lines Paul contrasts the Gentiles with
his race, the Jews. *Gentiles* occurred in the first line so it is not
stressed again here, and the contrast still works. Paul stresses *my*
but not *race.* The contrast is not in the idea of race but in the fact
that it's, in Paul's words, "**my** race." If you stress *race,* the contrast won't work at all. Race will sound like a new idea, but the
listeners need to hear that Paul's race is being contrasted with a
race that has been mentioned already. (In the last line, not stressing *ministry* helps the listener realize that it is a repeated idea, referring back to Paul's being "the apostle to the Gentiles," just the
thing that Paul glories in to make his race jealous.)

PARALLELISM 1:

For if **their** • **rejection** is the **reconciliation of the world,**
what will their **acceptance** be but **life from the dead?**
(Rom 11:15).

The parallelism is: rejection/reconciliation of the world along
with acceptance/life from the dead. All four ideas are new and all
are stressed.

PARALLELISM 2:

"**How** can you say, '**Show** us the **Father**'?
Do you not **believe** that **I** am **in** the Father and the **Father**
is in **me?**" (John 14:9-10).

The parallelism starts in the second line: I/Father—Father/me.
Of the four terms, stress only the first, third, and fourth. *Father*
occurs earlier in the passage so it's not stressed in the first half of

the parallelism, but it is stressed in the second half and so is *me*.
That's what makes it sound like a parallelism.

PARALLELISM 3:

When you **turn back** to him with **all your heart,** / to **do** what
is **right** before him, / Then **he** will turn back to **you**. . . .
(Tob 13:6).

Here the parallelism is: you/him—he/you. *He* and *you* in the
second half are stressed to bring out the parallelism even though
they are repetitions. The parallelism is clear even though there is
no stress on *you* or *him* in the first half.

Comparisons and parallelisms are common literary techniques in some parts of Scripture. Stress the compared or parallel
words in the second half. That's how the listener knows what is
happening.

RULE 8: Handle Repetitions

The rule to follow when a text refers to the same thing or person more than once is that you don't stress it after the first time—
with some exceptions as in Rule 7. Instead you stress new
information. Often you will find a repetition that uses different
words, so you have to watch carefully. In the next passage there
are three hidden repetitions, underlined, coming near the end.
Don't stress them.

Peter [**said**] to them,
"Repent and be **baptized, every one** of you,
in the **name** of **Jesus Christ** I for the **forgiveness** of your
    sins;
and you will **receive** the **gift** of the **holy Spirit.**
For the **promise** is made to **you** I and to your **children**
and to **all • those • far off,**
whomever the **Lord our God** will **call."**

He testified with many **other** arguments, and was **exhorting**
  them,
"Save yourselves from this **corrupt generation."**
Those who **accepted** his message I were **baptized** . . .
  (Acts 2:38-41).

The words *testified, arguments,* and *message* don't look like repetitions of anything previous, but they are. Peter has been giving
testimony and arguments and proclaiming a message all along,
and this was perfectly obvious to his listeners. Not stressing these
words will help make it obvious to your listeners as well. But the
fact that there were **other** arguments is something new, and so is
the fact that Peter was **exhorting** them and that some **accepted**
the message. Stress these three words.

The opposite of having the same idea in different words is
having different ideas but the same word. The rule says stress the
new idea even if the words are the same.

His **mercy** is from **age** to **age**
  to those who **fear** him (Luke 1:50).

Naturally you stress *age* both times here, and the reason is that
different ages are being named.

There is another kind of repetition. Sometimes an author
refers to the same thing in different ways and wants you to pay
special attention to the meaning that is added each time.

"I, the LORD, am your **God,**
  who **brought** you out of the **land of Egypt,** that **place of
  slavery** (Exod 20:2).

The underlining shows three words referring to God and two
phrases referring to Egypt, but each repetition adds an important
new meaning. In fact, their only point is to add new dimensions of
meaning. Poetry does this often, though here it's happening in prose.

The times, like the last two examples, when a repeated word or a second and third way of naming the same thing actually contain something new that needs stress are easy to recognize, but the opposite case is more difficult. Old information often hides in new words. You need to take care not to let these old ideas or information come across as something new. That will go a long way toward helping your listeners understand better some of Scripture's tough passages. Even if the words are different, don't stress them.

RULE 9: Distinguish Different Kinds of Questions

Probably we all have been taught in grade school reading lessons that we raise the pitch of our voices at the end of a question. That's partly right, but mostly wrong. It's right for questions that ask for a "yes" or "no" response but not for other questions. Questions that start with a question word, like *who*, *what*, *when*, *why*, have just about the same kind of pitch changes as an ordinary statement or a command.

Why • spend your **money** for what is not **bread** . . . ?
(Isa 55:2).

If you were to raise your voice at the end of this question, it might sound as if Jesus were about to give reasons why the apostles **should** spend their money on other things besides bread. Instead, think how Jesus would have pronounced the following:

Spend your **money** on **bread.**

Read the question with a similar intonation.

We do some interesting things with questions. There are questions that are more like exclamations or statements of fact. There are rhetorical questions:

What if I wish to give this **last** one the same as **you?**
(Matt 20:14).

There are questions where we don't wait for an answer but go right ahead and give the answer ourselves. There are questions that really are lists of choices, meant as complete lists. They have the pattern of a complete list with an upward inflection on the first item and a downward inflection on the last:

                  air,
  my way that is unfai-   **your**
Is it   or rather, are not
                                ways unfair?
(Ezek 18:25).

Keep in mind the purpose of a question as you decide how to read it.

RULE 10: Negatives and Pronouns Follow Their Own Odd Rules

Some words demand special treatment when it comes to stressing them or not. These include some negative words, words that refer to the speaker (*I*) or the one spoken to (*you*), and sometimes other pronouns.

Negatives. *Not* and *no* are important words, of course, and they are generally as new as anything else, but it is almost always better not to stress them. Instead, stress the verb or the other word that goes with the negative. Sometimes, though, there is a special reason to stress a negative. The next passage has two regular, unstressed negatives and one that is stressed.

[U]p to the time of the **law,** | **sin** was in the **world,**
though sin is not **accounted** when there is no law.
But **death • reigned** | from Adam to Moses,
even over those who did **not** sin . . . (Rom 5:13-14).

In the last line *not* is stressed because there sinning is an old idea. The word *even* tells us to expect something not just new but also unexpected, and that is contained in the word *not*. (You might have expected more stressed words in the second and third lines. But for Paul, the time "from Adam to Moses" is the same as the time "when there was no law," and that's the same idea as "up to the time of the law" in line one. You can help your listeners see it that way, too, by not stressing this repeated idea the second and third times.)

Speaker and spoken to. There needs to be a special reason for stressing words that refer to the one speaking or the person or persons being addressed. These usually are pronouns: *I, me, my, we, us, our, you, your.* Just being new is not enough reason to stress these words. Don't stress any of the underlined words in the following two passages.

> **Heed** me, I and you shall **eat well** . . . (Isa 55:2).
>
> **Shout** for **joy,** I O daughter Zion! (Zeph 3:14) ("Daughter Zion" = you).

There are occasions to stress these words, for example, when they occur in the second half (but not the first half) of comparisons or parallelisms (Rule 7), as in this parallelism:

> I will **take** you as my **own people,** and **you** shall have **me** as your **God** (Exod 6:7).

We stress words that refer to "you," the person being addressed, when they are first in a sentence and followed by a comma or a colon:

> **Brothers and sisters:**
> We **know** that **all things** • **work** for **good** I for those who **love** **God** . . . (Rom 8:28).

If *brothers and sisters* were later in the sentence, that phrase would not be stressed. Sometimes, however, several persons or things are addressed in turn. Then stress each one as it comes up.

Other pronouns. Other pronouns, like *he, him, she, her, they, them, it,* and even *that,* can be a little odd. They naturally refer to something or someone that has been mentioned already. Maybe it's because these words are repetitious by nature that sometimes they can break the rule that says, "don't stress repeated information."

"**Here** is a **true Israelite.** There is no **duplicity** in <u>**him**</u>" (John 1:47).

RULE 11: Stress Items That a Sentence Tells You to Stress

Sometimes a sentence or a special word in a sentence tells you what to stress. There are a number of ways this can happen. Sentences give words special prominence by moving them out of the place they normally have.

[I]f you are **patient** I when you **suffer** for **doing** what is
   good,
this is a **grace** before **God.**
For <u>**to this**</u> I you have been **called** (1 Pet 2:20-21).

The last line contains an unusual word order. The sentence is telling you to stress *this* by putting it at the beginning. Normally it would follow the verb and then it would not be stressed: "For you have been **called** to this." In either position it's tempting, but wrong, to stress the preposition *to*. It's also tempting to let your pitch rise while pronouncing *this*. Stick with the downward inflection. Start *this* with a higher pitch, but then come down.

Here's another way a sentence can order you to stress something:

Come, let us **return** to the LORD, / For <u>it is</u> **he** who has **rent,** but he will **heal** us . . . (Hos 6:1).

The phrase *it is* forces you to stress the next word. In this case, you might have wanted to stress *he*, anyway. Remember *he* is in that odd group of rule-breaking words that sometimes is stressed even though it's a repetition.

The helping verbs *does, do,* and *did* sometimes need stress. Their ordinary and unstressed use is in questions and negative sentences. In a positive sentence that is not a question, they are out of the ordinary. Then you need to stress these words, even when the main verb is not stressed:

I **do** believe.

It's almost never right to stress other helping verbs—examples are *may, might, would, could, should, have, has, had, am, are, was, were, will*—unless the main verb is also stressed, and not necessarily even then.

Intensive words, like *itself, yourself,* and *themselves* are stressed:

You have **seen** for **yourselves** I how I **treated** the **Egyptians** . . . (Exod 19:4).

A pronoun that immediately precedes one of these "self" words is stressed as well:

[A]ll **creation** is **groaning** in **labor** pains I **even until now;** and not only **that,** but **we ourselves,** who have the **first-fruits** of the **Spirit, we also** groan . . . (Rom 8:22-23).

This has about as many stress indicators as a sentence can handle! *Not only that, also,* and *ourselves* all tell you to stress *we.*

"Self" words have another use that is called reflexive. This just means that an action is reflecting back on the thing or person doing it, for example, hitting "yourself." It is not an intensive use, and these words are not necessarily stressed. Don't stress *yourselves* in the following passage:

Consequently, **you too** must **think** of yourselves as [being] **dead** to **sin** . . . (Rom 6:11).

This is a good sentence to try out different phrasing options. The comma wants you to put a pause after *consequently*. Try putting another pause after *too*. Then try another one after *yourselves*. Try skipping the pause after *yourselves* and adding one after *being* and another after *dead*. All of these options work and so does using no pauses at all.

If you will, take another break and turn to your Bible or a Lectionary. You will find opportunities to apply most of the rules above for reading like talk. Besides new information that needs stress and old information and unimportant words to leave unstressed, look for: items in a series, where usually you read each one as you would if it were alone; comparisons and parallelisms, where you stress the second half; repetitions that may be hidden but still should not be stressed. Decide how to deal with questions, negatives, and pronouns. Look for clues a sentence gives you by way of word order and intensive words. Be sure to read assertively, using the downward inflection often and avoiding a repetitive pattern. Don't fade away or lose energy just because you've come to the end of a sentence.

LESSON 3

You don't need to think about correct procedures when you are talking. It's a different situation when you are reading aloud. At this point you might even be thinking that the number of rules for reading like talk is overwhelming. Happily there's a priority among the rules, and some are more or less natural, in reading as in speaking. And here's another happy thought: The next set of rules starts with an opportunity for you to make your own exceptions to a rule.

RULE 12: Poetry and Rhetoric Give You More Choices

Repetition is sometimes used deliberately to add interest or to inspire the listeners. Martin Luther King's "I have a dream" speech used repetition. Fortunately, no rule for speech making required him to stress *dream* only the first time. Rhetorical and, especially, poetic speech makes plentiful use of repetition. We don't so much need to, but we want to pay special attention to the repeated ideas each time.

"The **God** of my **gladness** and **joy**" is repetitious and poetic. Here's another example:

> The **sun** will be **turned** to **darkness**
>   and the **moon** I to **blood,**
> At the **coming** of the **day of the Lord,**
>   the **great** and **terrible day** (Joel 3:4).

In the last line it seems that greatness and terribleness are the new things and that you should stress these words and not *day*. But really nothing in the last line is new. The whole line is another way of saying "day of the Lord." Poetry and oratory love repetition, and often it's effective just to read each part as if it were brand new. So stress *great*, *terrible*, **and** *day*.

> Among the **nations' idols** is there **any** that gives **rain?**
> Or can the **mere heavens** send **showers?** (Jer 14:22).

Rain and showers are the same thing for the poet. Even if the word *rain* were repeated, in poetry you could stress it both times. Use an upward inflection at the ends of these yes-no questions.

In poetry you have some freedom to choose. The next passage repeats the idea of banishing. Would you stress it or not the second time?

> He shall **banish** the **chariot** from **Ephraim,**
>   and the **horse** I from **Jerusalem;**
> The **warrior's bow** shall be banished . . . (Zech 9:10).

The creation story of the Easter Vigil, with its days of creation, can be read like an ordinary story, stressing words like *evening*, *morning*, and *day* only the first time they occur:

Thus **evening** came and **morning** • **followed**—the **first** •
day. . . .
Evening came and morning followed—the **second** day . . .
third day . . . and so on. . . (Gen 1:5ff.).

But it can also be read poetically. The underlining shows repeated
words that can be stressed in a poetic reading.

Thus **evening** came and **morning** • **followed**—the **first** •
day . . .
<u>Evening</u> came and <u>**morning** • **followed**</u>—the second • <u>day</u>
. . . **third** • <u>day</u> . . . and so on.

The number of evenings, mornings, and days is so small at this
point in the story of the world, it seems somehow appropriate to
emphasize these words each time. Besides, this story is also about
the creation of the names of things.

You can use some originality and a sense of play when reading poetry. Remember that poetry gives you options, so don't let
the verse form determine how you read. For example, if it doesn't
make good sense to pause at the end of a line, then don't. (Even
in more familiar poetry where lines rhyme, you need to decide
whether pausing at the end of a line makes sense.)

RULE 13: Stress Two or More Words in a Row

Here's a common situation: You have noun—a name for
something—and a word in front of it that describes that thing.
Usually when this happens both the noun and the modifier (describing word) have their independent meanings, for example:

many-colored coat

The coat is described as many-colored. These are independent ideas,
separate bits of information. If both are new ideas, then you stress
them both. The noun gets a little more stress than the modifier.

The problem is that it's easy to omit the stress on one or the other. Stressing two words in a row doesn't seem to fit our preconceived notions about rhythm. But talking doesn't have preconceived ideas about rhythm. There can be two stresses in a row or more. It happens often with nouns and modifiers ("your mortal bodies" in the next passage) and, as you can see, in other places in a sentence as well.

> If the **Spirit** of the one who **raised** • **Jesus** from the **dead** •
>   **dwells** in you,
> the one who raised Christ from the dead
> will **give life** to **your** • **mortal** • **bodies** • **also** . . . (Rom 8:11).

Here's another telling example. Take this short sentence nice and slow:

> Then **God** • **delivered** • **all** • **these** • **commandments** . . .
>   (Exod 20:1).

RULE 14: Combine and Separate

There are many situations where you have to be careful either to keep words together or to set them apart. Sometimes words that are separated on the page actually belong together and need to sound that way. Combining and separating are important skills for the reader. Here are some cases organized into various categories.

Compound nouns. A describing word may be so closely connected to the noun following it that the two words function as one. Sometimes they're written as one word, sometimes separately, sometimes as one word with a hyphen. These are compound nouns. Read them as if they were one word, even if they are written as two words. The major stress is almost always on the first word or part, whether it seems to make sense or not. The second might not be stressed at all. Sometimes it is stressed but less than the first. Stressing the second part equally or more than the first, makes it sound funny or mean something different. Here are some examples:

evildoer—not necessarily a doer who is evil (**evil doer**),
but a doer of evil

dwelling places—not places that dwell (**dwelling places**),
but places where people dwell
sheepfold, **foot**steps, **meat**ball, **ball** game

. . . they **devoted** themselves to **meeting together** in the
temple area . . . (Acts 2:46).

Temple area here is a compound noun. Keep it together and stress
temple, not *area.*

These are not compound nouns: *paralyzed people, crippled
people, possessed people.* Put at least equal stress on *people* if
"people" is a new idea. After all, we are people first. *Eagle wings*
is a compound noun; stress the first word. *Eagle's wings* is not;
stress both words or whichever is new. *Stone hearts* is not a compound
noun. Many, but not all, compound names of places are exceptions
to the rule and have the main stress on the last part:
Mount Sinai, Stone Mountain.

Single units of meaning. Here is a group of four words that
need to be kept together:

[A] **just • savior** is he,
Meek, and **riding on an ass** . . . (Zech 9:9).

Just and *savior* need that bit of separation that gives each its own
identity. *Riding on an ass* is quite different. It's not an ordinary
phrase; it's one unit of meaning. You don't even begin to get the
meaning of what Jesus is doing until the phrase is complete. I indicate
a phrase that needs to be kept together because it comprises
just one unit of meaning by using bold print for the entire phrase
with no separating dots. Of course, you don't stress unimportant
words in the phrase—just as you don't stress all the syllables of a
single, longer word. Sometimes being extra quick with the phrase,
as if it were all one word, helps to keep it together. Always save
the downward inflection until the end.

Remember, giving a phrase a downward inflection at the end does not mean that its ending word gets less stress. It gets two pitches, starting high (like the rest of the phrase) and ending lower:

riding on an aa-
               ass

Keeping together phrases that are a single unit of meaning can be very important, for example:

Now when they **heard** this, they were **cut to the heart** . . .
(Acts 2:37).

If you separate *cut* from *to the heart*, it will sound as if they were cut literally.

Sometimes you find a single unit of meaning in words that are separated. "Taking aside" is such a unit in the next example:

Then **Peter** • **took** Jesus **aside** and began to **rebuke** him . . .
(Matt 16:22).

Read *took* and *aside* with similar stress and pitch and they will sound like one. The word *Jesus* might have required stress, too, if it had been new. In that case, since you couldn't keep Jesus' name separate by difference in stress, you would have had to do it by taking a little extra time before and after *Jesus*. As it is, though, Jesus was mentioned in an earlier part of the passage that was not quoted. That makes it easier to read than it would have been otherwise.

Phrases that are units of meaning are quite common. Watch for them as you prepare a reading.

All the day I am an **object of laughter;**
   everyone • **mocks** me (Jer 20:7).

To identify them you can only go by your own judgment and understanding.

Should a man **nourish anger** against his fellows
and **expect • healing** from the **LORD?** (Sir 28:3).

Nourish anger and *expect healing* are both verb-noun phrases, but
I would call the first a single unit of meaning—you don't know
anything about it until it's complete—and not the second.

Separators. *And* (along with the commas that stand for *and*
in a series) almost always separates. It says: "Here are different
things." Read them that way.

They **ate** their **meals** with **exultation** ∣ and **sincerity of
heart** (Acts 2:46).

A pause can help you make exultation and sincerity of heart
sound like two "things." Be sure to pronounce each with a downward inflection. Remember it's a series, and since it's not a complete list, pronounce each as you would if it were the only one.
"Sincerity of heart" is another single unit of meaning so save the
downward inflection for the last word:

```
     ta-                    hea-
exul-     |        cerity of
     tion   and sin-           art
```

There are rare cases where *and* does not separate simply because it comes in the middle of a phrase that functions like a
single word. This is an example:

a **land • flowing** with **milk and honey** (Num 14:8).

Or is a separator also, and it has its own unusual cases like
the following:

a people so **vast** that it cannot be **numbered or counted**
(1 Kgs 3:8).

Being numbered and being counted are not two different things,
so read them together.

Longer phrases. Sometimes one piece of information has several meaningful parts, and it takes a longer phrase to make it complete. Then it's important not to break it up with a pause and a downward inflection. Keeping these longer phrases together is another way of being kind to your listener. It enables the listener to deal with a smaller number of chunks of meaning and makes difficult passages easier to grasp.

Here is a passage with an unusually large number of long phrases. I marked some possible pause places with a vertical line. I numbered and underlined the longer phrases.

Blessed be (1) the **God** and **Father** of our **Lord Jesus Christ**, | who in his **great mercy** | **gave** us a **new birth** | to a **living hope** | (2) through the **resurrection** of **Jesus Christ** from the **dead**, | (3) to an **inheritance** that is **imperishable**, | **undefiled**, | and **unfading**, | **kept** in **heaven** for **you** who by the **power** of **God** | are **safeguarded** | through **faith** | (4) to a **salvation** that is **ready** to be **revealed** in the **final time** (1 Pet 1:3-5).

Many words in a typical sentence get a downward inflection, but save the downward inflection for the end of a phrase. It signals the end of that idea. The last phrase, "to a salvation . . . time," is very long, and it could be broken up with slight pauses or slow-downs and slight downward inflections as long as a more pronounced downward inflection comes at the end. Notice in phrase 3 that *imperishable*, *undefiled* and *unfading* are separated. There must be pauses within this phrase because it contains this series of three separate items. It is not meant to be complete series, so each one gets a downward inflection.

We can begin to understand all of these phrases right away, so they're not single units of meaning; but all their words are necessary to tell us exactly what is meant. We know "God and Father" (phrase 1), but we don't know whose God and Father it is yet. We don't know right away which "resurrection," which "inheritance," which "salvation." Interrupting these phrases with a downward

inflection would signal, incorrectly, that now we know what we
need to know and the words that follow are unimportant extras.

Sometimes the person telling the story does give unneeded
information:

> He **left Nazareth** and **went** to **live** in **Capernaum** | by the
> **sea,** | in the **region** of **Zebulun** and **Naphtali** (Matt 4:13).

Capernaum is (or was, anyway) a well-known place; by itself it
tells exactly where Jesus went. The two following phrases are
extra information. It makes sense to use a downward inflection on
Capernaum and pause slightly. Do the same with *sea* but with a
slighter pause.

It's not necessary to hurry through a longer phrase to keep it
together. Just save your downward inflection for the last word in
the phrase. Some Bible sentences get very long, and the more parts
a sentence has, the harder it is to understand. Paying attention to
phrasing can reduce the number of parts your listeners need to
keep track of and keep some Bible sentences from challenging
people more than they need to.

Associations. Finally, sometimes you have to help the listeners know where a word or phrase fits with other words in a
sentence. This is true especially when a word or phrase associates
with two other words at the same time.

> For the **gifts** | and the **call** | of **God** | are **irrevocable**
> (Rom 11:29).

You need to help your reader understand that the gifts and the
call are two different things and that they both are God's. Pause after
gifts to separate the two items. Then pause again after *call* to make
of God connect with both of them. A final and slightly longer pause
after *God* helps the listener associate *irrevocable* with *gifts* and *call*
and not directly with *God*. If you could take either *gifts*, *call*, or *God*
out of this sentence, you wouldn't need any of these pauses.

Here's an example where intonation is important:

For it is **he** who has **rent,** but he will **heal** us . . . (Hos 6:1).

Us goes with both *rent* and *heal.* (God does both of those things to us.) Pause after rent, but not the kind of pause that makes it sound like a complete idea. It's not complete without *us.* The downward inflection, which comes at the end of most phrases, signals completion, so don't use it here, or use only a slight downward nod.

Here's one last example. It shows that you sometimes have to put a pause in an unusual place:

[H]e **foresaw** I and **spoke of** I the **resurrection** of the
    Messiah . . . (Acts 2:31).

David "foresaw" the resurrection of the Messiah, and he also "spoke of" it. *Of* does not go with *foresaw,* and that's why *of* needs to be kept close together with *spoke.* Normally you wouldn't pause after a preposition like *of,* but here you have to. Without this pause listeners won't hear that the Messiah's resurrection was "foreseen" as well as "spoken of."

Combining and separating words is part of the way English makes sense. Often it's fairly obvious to both reader and listener, but getting this right consistently is a challenge. If you don't read so that your listeners can hear the meaning, they might with some effort understand you anyway. But this is something that makes the lector's job important—the Word of God has more power over us when we simply hear it than when we figure it out.

RULE 15: Signal Quotations

You can't make quotation marks in the air when reading a person's exact words in the Liturgy of the Word, but there is another way of signaling quotations. Between a word like *say* and the actual quotation there usually is a comma although some passages use a colon instead. Almost any other time commas signal the end of a phrase and a downward inflection, but with quotations those commas should be read more like colons, which don't mean an ending but "look at what's coming next." This is a place for a pause. There may or may not be a slight drop in pitch but not anything like an ending. This pause, with perhaps a slight pitch change, signals that a quotation is coming.

> "A **man** had **two sons.**
> He came to the **first** and **said,** [pause]
> **'Son, go out** I and **work** in the **vineyard** today.'
> He said in reply, [pause] 'I will **not**'" (Matt 21:28-29).

When you begin reading a quotation of a person's exact words, you usually start over the process of determining what is new and needs stress. In a story an idea that is repeated may count as new the second time if it's spoken by different characters in two different situations or even by the same character in different situations or by a character and the narrator. An example is found in this continuation of the above passage.

> . . . but **afterwards** [he] **changed** his **mind** I and **went.**
> The man came to the **other** son I and gave the **same order**
> (Matt 21:29-30).

The order had been given once before so the idea of order is not new, but before it was in the father's voice. Here it's in the narrator's voice and it's new to the narrator so it should be stressed.

A word inside a quotation may need to be stressed even if the same word occurred just before the quotation:

> "[M]**any peoples** shall **come** and **say:**
> "**Come,** let us **climb** the LORD's **mountain,**
> to the **house** of the **God** of **Jacob** . . ." (Isa 2:3).

In Scripture you occasionally find a quotation in which a familiar text or a familiar saying is quoted. Here is a passage with some sayings about a cornerstone:

Therefore, its **value** is for **you** who have **faith,** but for those
without faith:
*"The stone that the **builders rejected***
has become the **cornerstone,"**
and
*"A stone that will make people **stumble,***
and a **rock** *that will make them* **fall"** (1 Pet 2:7-8).

The colon, quotation marks, italics, and line breaks are all visual
clues in the Lectionary that tell you these are quotations. Your listeners have only your voice. A significant pause and only a slight
downward inflection after the colon will help listeners identify the
first of the coming quotations. The word "and," standing on a line
by itself, encourages you to pause again and make the next lines
sound like another familiar saying.

When you read a person's exact words you have all the more
reason for reading like talk. The emotion in a character's words,
even if they are God's, should come across in your voice. That is
not being too dramatic. If there is more than one speaker in a
story, it is not necessary to devise different sounding voices for
each of them. Make your one voice carry the different emotions
that different characters feel. That's enough to distinguish one
character from another.

RULE 16: Keep Parenthetical Remarks Parenthetical

A parenthetical remark is by design a phrase that is not
stressed, even if it contains new material. It's an aside, spoken in
a lowered tone.

For it is **better** to **suffer** for doing **good,**
if that be the will of God, than for doing **evil** (1 Pet 3:17).

"If that be the will of God" is a parenthetical remark. Usually parenthetical remarks are set off by commas.

RULE 17: Savor the Sounds of English

English has a wide variety of sounds. Other languages may have more characters, but hardly any other language has as many sounds as English. English is full of consonants, soft ones and hard ones. You can think of English as a harsh-sounding language. By comparison, Spanish or Japanese sounds are much softer. To become proficient at reading orally in English, you almost have to enjoy the beauty, the sometimes harsh beauty, of English consonants.

You have to work at pronouncing English. All those consonant sounds must be heard. Making your reading "like talk" doesn't mean making it like everyday, careless talk. When people hear you in conversation, there almost always are clues in the situation that both of you are engaged in that help them understand the sounds that come from your mouth. When people hear you read, no such clues are available. Their understanding depends entirely on what their ears tell them. That means clear diction is important. It can also be fun and an interesting challenge. What other language can put as many as five consonant sounds together in one word without a vowel sound between!

Rules for consonants. Make sure your *d*'s sound different from your *t*'s, and your *b*'s from your *p*'s. Let your listeners hear the final consonants of words. You have to finish a final consonant before starting the next word. You can do this by "letting go" of the consonant sound at the end of one word before starting on the next. Open your lips again after closing them on an *m*, *b*, *d*, or *g*. Release some air after a *p*, *t*, or *k*. Or there's another way. We often run words together without taking a break. Just make sure your final consonants don't sound like the beginning of the next word. Sometimes it helps to make a final consonant last a little longer than other consonants. Sometimes, especially with *s*'s, which last longer anyway, a slight interruption in the air flow works. Be especially careful if the final consonant could combine with the next word and make a new and unwanted word, as in "Let us pray." Stop the air flow after *s*. You can do it without pausing.

Rules for vowels. English has only five vowels—and sometimes *y*—just like many other languages, but the sounds those five vowels can make number a lot more than that. Make sure your accented short *e*'s, *a*'s, and *i*'s are all different. Try saying, "and in the end." You should notice changes in the shape of your mouth. Make sure your *ah*'s and *aw*'s are different; feel the different shapes of your mouth. Say, "the Father of Waters." On the other hand, unaccented short vowels often are indistinguishable from one another. Say, "nation, heaven, people, Galileans, Elamites, Mesopotamia." The vowel sound in the underlined syllables is called "schwa." Don't over pronounce, or fret over how to pronounce, all those unaccented vowels. They're very quick.

RULE 18: Try This Pronunciation Shortcut

People who read aloud may wonder what to do when the same consonant ends one word and begins the next word. They want to use clear diction, but they don't want to sound silly. The song "You've Got to be Taught," from the musical *South Pacific*, illustrates the problem. The Broadway actor did a great job of pronouncing both *t*'s of "got to" without over pronouncing them or sounding silly. He pronounced the beginning of the first *t*, but he didn't end it. He just stopped without letting any air out. Then, since his tongue was already in *t* position, he was able to proceed to the end of the second *t*. There was a slight pause in the middle (very slight), so it sounded like two *t*'s; but really it was more like one and a half, a kind of stretched out, or supersized, *T*.

Over pronouncing "got to" will make the phrase sound like three syllables when it should be two: "got—(air released)—to." (Try it.) If the phrase is under pronounced, *got* will sound like "gah," without any final consonant. The correct way is in the middle between the silly one and the lazy one: "You've got (stop) to be taught."

This technique is not necessary for double consonants within a word, which are pronounced as one consonant. There are a lot of instances where the procedure can be used, however, including cases where the two adjacent consonants are not identical but are pronounced with the same movement of the tongue or lips. It's not always necessary to use the supersizing technique, especially if you can pronounce the entire two adjacent consonants without producing an extra syllable between them or if it's a place where a pause makes sense.

Here are some phrases to practice on. The supersizing procedure means there is a stop but not a release of air between the two identical or similar consonant sounds. The alternative is to pronounce the first consonant, let go, and then pronounce the second.

with the
said to
sheep by name
called together
if found
same mind
from East to West
returned to (Supersizing doesn't work for me on this one.
   I'd pause after *returned.*)
Send down (You can't supersize the *d,* but you can lengthen
   the *n* in *send,* and it works.)

Several consonants together don't necessarily mean you can shorten or combine any of them. Pronounce all of these consonants completely:

Hellenists complained
and bring
breaststroke

Correct diction is important in reading like talk, even though we often talk imprecisely. Adding energy to those consonants, making sure we hear all of them, will not make your reading sound any less like talk, especially if you take advantage of Rule 18 when it works for you.

Summary

Most of the instructions in this guide follow from the conviction that the readings proclaimed in the Liturgy of the Word, or any oral reading, should sound "like talk" in all the varieties that talking has. It should follow the same patterns that we hear people using in ordinary conversation or storytelling. It should be as meaningful as when people speak their minds. A total of eighteen rules spelled out how to make this happen. It's not a complete list, but it is a lot to remember. Reading like talk, however, is less daunting than that would suggest. There's a priority, with the downward inflection and stressing what's new being high on the list. Here is a condensed version that puts most of the above rules into a few categories:

- **Mean what you say.** You can make your reading sound as if you mean what you say by using a downward inflection often—at the ends of most phrases and on some other words as well. An upward inflection, anything more than a slight lift at the end of some downward inflections, is appropriate for only a few situations like the end of a yes-no question and the first item of a complete list. Don't get stuck in either a monotone or a repetitive pattern of pitch.

- **Use stressed and unstressed words.** Deciding which words to stress is the biggest part of preparing to read like talk. Stress new information. Leave unstressed the old information and noninformative words like helping verbs and most prepositions. Stress lots of words of many kinds—nouns, verbs, adjectives, etc.—as many as half of the words in some paragraphs. But often these are followed by passages with only a few stresses. Be suspicious if you start getting a regular stress pattern. Stress the second half of a comparison or a parallel construction even if it's old information. Sentences can tell you to stress something by certain words or phrases as well as unusual word order. Poetry and rhetoric often allow you to use stress where plain prose would not. Don't let the ends of sentences fade away. Often the most important ideas are there.

• **Organize words and phrases logically.** Your listeners should hear together things that belong together and hear separate things that are separate. Saving the downward inflection for the end of a phrase is the way to keep it together. Speeding up can help but only for very short phrases, especially phrases that are single units of meaning. Commas and the words *and* and *or* are almost always separators. In the majority of cases a series of items is an incomplete list. Pronounce each item as if it were the only one. Words that belong together logically are not always found right next to each other. You can make them sound together by using similar pitch and stress. When a word or phrase belongs with two or more other words, pauses can help you make the connections.

• **Savor the sounds of English.** Lastly, even though we don't always do it in ordinary speech, be sure to pronounce all of the many sounds English has to offer, especially the consonants and, among these, especially consonants that end a word. Even when there are four or five consonants in a row, pronounce them all. If the same or a similar consonant ends one word and begins the next word, it's often best not to pronounce both of them completely. Combine the two with just a little stop between.

Putting It All Together

Here are some longer readings from the Lectionary. Use them to try out what you have learned about reading like talk. You've seen most of the first selection already. Before you try reading it out loud, make some decisions about how to read it. Which words should be stressed, and which words, though perhaps important, are repetitions or synonyms that don't need stress?

Which combinations of words are single units of meaning, and how do the sentences divide into phrases? Are there any lists or series of items, any complete lists?

> Then Peter stood up with the Eleven,
> raised his voice, and proclaimed to them. . . .
> "Therefore let the whole house of Israel know for certain
> that God has made him both Lord and Messiah,
> this Jesus whom you crucified."
> Now when they heard this, they were cut to the heart,
> and they asked Peter and the other apostles,
> "What are we to do, my brothers?" (Acts 2:14, 36-37).

Think about how you would "tell" this passage before going on to read about how I would prepare it.

As I prepare to read this passage, I would first notice how different the rhythms of the two paragraphs are. In the first paragraph everything is new, and literally half of the words need the listeners' special attention. In the second paragraph there are only a few new ideas to stress, namely, *heard, cut to the heart, asked,* and *do.*

Stood up, house of Israel, and *cut to the heart* are examples of word groups that need to be read almost like one word. "Whole house of Israel" is a phrase with two parts. Separate *whole* from *house of Israel* but keep the phrase together by saving the downward inflection until the last word. In the phrase "asked Peter and the other apostles," *asked* is the only new and stressed word so the downward inflection starts already with *Peter.*

The end of a sentence usually is not the place to slow down or get quieter. *Crucified* at the end of the first paragraph is a very intense word.

Repeated ideas do not always come back in the same words. *Other apostles* is not stressed because it refers to the same group as *the eleven.*

"Both Lord and Christ" sounds to me like a complete list. It's as if God couldn't have done any more for Jesus than make him Lord and Christ. Pronouncing *Lord* with a higher pitch and *Christ* with a lower, declining pitch works here. The first two lines contain another series—three things that Peter did. This one is an incomplete list; each item gets a downward inflection.

Finally, in the phrase *cut to the heart* the same consonant ends one word and begins the next. It is very hard to sound natural when reading "cut to" without using Rule 18. In other words, take a shortcut; combine the two *t*'s into one, but supersize it. There should be a very short stop after *cut* but no release of air; then continue with *to*.

Putting it together, I would read the passage like this:

Then **Peter • stood up** with the **Eleven,**
raised his **voice,** and **proclaimed** to them. . . .
"Therefore let the **whole • house of Israel | know** for **certain**
that **God** has **made** him both **Lord** and **Messiah,**
this **Jesus** whom you **crucified.**"
Now when they **heard** this, they were **cut to the heart,**
and they **asked** Peter and the other apostles,
"What are we to **do,** my brothers?" (Acts 2:14, 36-37).

The next passage contains several quotations. Remember the comma that precedes a quotation is not an ending but a sign that says, "Look at what's coming next." This passage has a lot of *and*'s—a word that usually, but not always, separates. In most cases you can tell the meaning best by giving what comes before *and* its own identity. Try using a downward inflection and maybe a slight pause.

"What is your opinion?
A man had two sons.
He came to the first and said,
'Son, go out and work in the vineyard today.'
He said in reply, 'I will not,'
but afterwards he changed his mind and went.
The man came to the other son and gave the same order.
He said in reply, 'Yes, sir,' but did not go.
Which of the two did his father's will?"

They answered, "The first."
Jesus said to them, "Amen, I say to you,
tax collectors and prostitutes
are entering the kingdom of God before you.
When John came to you in the way of righteousness,
you did not believe him;
but tax collectors and prostitutes did.
Yet even when you saw that,
you did not later change your minds and believe him"
    (Matt 21:28-32).

Here is how I would plan this reading with some explanations interspersed. Some of the phrases, marked by vertical lines, are very short. They still benefit from a pause and a downward inflection.

Jesus said to the **chief priests** and **elders** of the **people:** No
    need for pauses here. Priests and elders can be thought of as one
    group. But use a downward inflection on both *priests* and *elders*.
"**What** is your **opinion?** No stress on *your*. Downward inflection
    on *opinion*.
A **man** had **two sons.**
He came to the **first** and **said,**
'**Son, go out** | and **work** in the **vineyard** today.' Pausing after
    out helps keep *work in the vineyard* together.
He said in reply, 'I will **not,**' The main verb is unspoken, so *not*
    gets the stress.
but **afterwards • changed** his **mind** | and **went.** *Mind* is as new
    as anything and needs stress.
The man came to the **other** son | and gave the **same order.**
    The word *order* can be thought of as a repetition, but it is new for
    the narrator's voice, so it should be stressed.
He said in reply, '**Yes,** sir,' but did not **go.** *Go* is the main verb
    and gets stress rather than *not*.
Which of the **two • did** his **father's will?**" It's easy to over-
    look *did*, but it's a main verb here. Stress it. The idea of *father* and

will occurred previously in the story, but at this point the story is over, and Jesus is speaking in his own voice. He would stress these two words.

They answered, "The **first.**"

Jesus said to them, "**Amen**, I **say** to you,

tax collectors | and **prostitutes** *Tax collectors* (a compound noun, stress on the first part) and "prostitutes" are two separate groups. Separating them is better than lumping them together.

are **entering** the **kingdom of God** before **you.** *Kingdom of God* is a single unit of meaning. *You* is the second item of a contrast (with *tax collectors* and *prostitutes*) and needs stress. *Before* does not need stress, but if you do stress it, stress *you* even more.

When **John** • **came** to you in the way of **righteousness,** Stress *John* and *came.* Separate these two words, and put "came to you" together.

you did not **believe** him;

but **tax** collectors and **prostitutes** • **did.**

Yet even when you saw **that,**

you did not later **change** your **minds** | and **believe** him" (Matt 21:28-32). Changing one's mind is an important thing to do. The chief priests and elders should have changed their minds like the first son in the story. Even though the idea of changing minds came up before in the story, it counts as a new idea here because Jesus is now speaking for himself and not as the narrator or a character in the story.

One final reading:

Seek the LORD while he may be found,
    call him while he is near.
Let the scoundrel forsake his way,
    and the wicked man his thoughts;
Let him turn to the LORD for mercy;
    to our God, who is generous in forgiving.
For my thoughts are not your thoughts,
    nor are your ways my ways, says the LORD.

As high as the heavens are above the earth,
so high are my ways above your ways
and my thoughts above your thoughts (Isa 55:6-9).

Plan how you would read this one, and then see if the stresses and pauses indicated below make sense to you? Do you agree with them?

Seek the LORD | while he may be **found,**
call him | while he is **near.**
Let the **scoundrel** • **forsake** his **way,**
and the **wicked** man his **thoughts;**
Let him **turn** to the LORD for **mercy;**
to our **God,** who is **generous** in **forgiving.**
For **my thoughts** are not **your** thoughts,
nor are your **ways** • **my** ways, says the LORD.
As **high** as the **heavens** are above the **earth,**
so high are **my ways** above **your** ways
and my **thoughts** above **your** thoughts (Isa 55:6-9).

Conclusion

Think of these lessons on reading like talk as a travel guide on what is sure to be a long trip. It's a fascinating journey, and there's more to see than what's in the guide.

You are helping people celebrate the Good News of God. You want to stir up their memories, reawaken their understanding, and enliven their faith by what you read. The first thing to do is to try to understand the reading yourself, but that's only the beginning. You have to decide how to read so others will understand, remember, and, perhaps, be convinced.

Reading doesn't come naturally to us as talking does, and talking is the medium that people understand best. It's their first language. Talking is what people remember best, and talking is believable because it sounds like something the person speaking actually believes. God chose to reveal the Good News in language that people were familiar with. That is why you need to overcome the artificial nature of reading and make your reading sound "like talk." With practice it can be done. The rules described and illustrated here can help you. Hopefully, you'll learn even more on your own. This is a learning process that you never finish.

When my children were young, I would read to them stories that had many pictures and few words; but the reading challenged me, and I enjoyed it. When they asked me to read a story that I had read often before, that was another challenge. The way children feel about their stories is a good analogy for the People of God and the Word of God. "Read it again," children say, and it's a delight every time. God's people never tire of their stories, either.

That's true for me, whether I am celebrating the Liturgy of the Word in the midst of the people or taking the role of lector and whether or not I've heard or read these selections before.

You do a lot of work in the process of having any good celebration, but it's never so good that from then on all you want to do is repeat what's been done. It's not that something went wrong before, but that following rules and getting it right are only the beginnings of making a celebration. Along with that comes something like style and letting the spirit of the occasion—or, with liturgical celebrations, the Spirit in the words of God—move you.

Bibliography

Bowen, Elbert R. and others. *Communicative Reading*, Fourth Edition. New York: Macmillan Publishing Co., Inc., 1978.

Rosser, Aelred R. *Workbook for Lectors and Gospel Readers.* Chicago: Liturgy Training Publications, 2001.

Wallace, James A. *The Ministry of Lectors.* Collegeville: The Liturgical Press, 1981.